GALE
CENGAGE Learning

Novels for Students, Volume 39

Project Editor: Sara Constantakis **Rights Acquisition and Management**: Margaret Chamberlain-Gaston, Jacqueline Flowers **Composition**: Evi Abou-El-Seoud **Manufacturing**: Rhonda Dover

Imaging: John Watkins

Product Design: Pamela A. E. Galbreath, Jennifer Wahi **Content Conversion**: Katrina Coach **Product Manager**: Meggin Condino © 2012 Gale, Cengage Learning

For product information and technology assistance, contact us at **Gale Customer Support, 1-800-877-4253**.
For permission to use material from this text or product, submit all requests online at **www.cengage.com/permissions**.
Further permissions questions can be emailed to **permissionrequest@cengage.com** While every effort has been made to ensure the reliability of the information presented in this publication, Gale, a part of Cengage Learning, does not guarantee the accuracy of the data contained herein. Gale accepts no payment for listing; and inclusion in the publication of any organization, agency, institution, publication, service, or individual does not imply endorsement of the editors or publisher. Errors brought to the attention of the publisher and verified to the satisfaction of the publisher will be corrected in future editions.

Gale 27500 Drake Rd.
Farmington Hills, MI, 48331-3535

ISBN-13: 978-1-4144-6702-3
ISBN-10: 1-4144-6702-8
ISSN 1094-3552

This title is also available as an e-book.

ISBN-13: 978-1-4144-7368-0
ISBN-10: 1-4144-7368-0
Contact your Gale, a part of Cengage Learning sales representative for ordering information.

Printed in Mexico
1 2 3 4 5 6 7 16 15 14 13 12

American Born Chinese

Gene Luen Yang 2006

Introduction

Gene Luen Yang's graphic novel, *American Born Chinese*, was originally serialized online on *Modern Tales.com*. First Second Books published the complete story in print in 2006. *American Born Chinese* has the distinction of being the first graphic novel to receive the Michael L. Printz Award and was the first graphic novel to be nominated for the National Book Award. The full text is no longer available online. Yang, however, does provide a preview on his home page (http://geneyang.com/american-born-chinese).

American Born Chinese contains three

seemingly unrelated narratives that are creatively linked together in the end. The book begins with an account of the Monkey King, a traditional Chinese folktale. It then details the life of Jin Wang, a Chinese American boy who moves to a predominately Caucasian suburb. The final story concerns the Caucasian American Danny and his cousin Chin-Kee. Chin-Kee is a negative Asian stereotype who makes life difficult for his cousin. Each thread of the graphic novel is drawn into an exciting conclusion that explores themes of self-identity and self-acceptance.

Author Biography

Yang was born in Alameda, California, in 1973. Yang describes his childhood in the California suburb of Saratoga as complex in his Kartika *Review* interview with Sunny Woan. He saw Saratoga gradually shift from a predominately Caucasian population into a diverse neighborhood that came to include people and cultures from around the globe. The child of Asian immigrants, Yang grew up listening to traditional stories from China such as the Monkey King, which he later included in his graphic novel. He graduated from the University of California at Berkeley with a degree in computer science and a minor in creative writing.

Yang began drawing comics while he was in elementary school. Yang created Humble Comics in 1996 as a vehicle to publish his work. In 1997, he won a Xeric grant to create *Gordon Yamamoto and the King of the Geeks*. Yang has created comics with different themes over the years, including *The Rosary Comic Book*, which incorporates religious themes that reflect the artist's personal beliefs. Many of his other comics are more fantasy-based. Yang self-published some of his early work and serialized other stories, including *American Born Chinese*, online.

The print publication of *American Born Chinese* in its entirety in 2006 brought the author mainstream popularity as he addressed the issues of multiculturalism, assimilation, and identity. He followed this success with a 2009 collaboration with Derek Kirk Kim, *The Eternal Smile*. Yang published *Prime Baby* in 2010 and worked with Thien Pham on the 2011 comic *Level Up*. Several of Yang's comic tales have received the Eisner Award, which is considered the Academy Award for American comic writers.

As of 2011, Yang lived in Fremont, California, with his wife and children. When he was not creating comics, Yang teaches computer science at the Catholic high school Bishop OLaDowd in Oakland, California. He is also a strong supporter of using comics in education.

Plot Summary

American Born Chinese is a multi-narrative work that develops the three distinct stories of the Monkey King, Jin Wang, and Danny and Chin-Kee. Yang unites these stories at the conclusion. The three narratives are broken into different sections of the book that resemble chapters. As a graphic novel, *American Born Chinese* tells the stories using sequential art.

Media Adaptations

- Yang explains the concepts behind *American Born Chinese* in a YouTube video posted by the America.gov Web site on June 4, 2009.

- Yang discusses his work in a lecture

Individual pictures or panels are created to depict moments. The panels are placed in sequence to drive the action of the story, and the text supports the graphics. The square boxes hold narrative text, and the balloons have dialogue or thoughts. The text is written in capital letters so that it is easier to read. A page featuring a character's picture introduces his chapter of the book.

Monkey King

This multi-narrative story begins with the modern retelling of the Monkey King, a centuries-old Chinese fable. The first scene is told by an omniscient narrator and describes a banquet of the gods in heaven. The Monkey King smells the food and becomes hungry. Born out of a rock, he is a "Deity in his own right" and rules the monkeys on Flower-Fruit Mountain. He has also mastered Kung-Fu and the four heavenly disciplines to become immortal. The Monkey King decides he should attend the banquet of the gods in heaven because he is a deity. The gods, however, refuse to associate with him because he is a monkey and does not wear shoes. The Monkey King is insulted and forced to leave. In retaliation, he attacks the guests at the party. When he returns to Flower-Fruit Mountain, however, he feels ashamed of being a monkey. The anger and shame he feels as a result of the rejection of the other gods will affect his future actions.

Jin

Jin Wang begins the story of his life in his first section of the graphic novel. The story begins with Jin's mother telling him a Chinese parable as the family drives to their new home. Jin plays with a Transformer toy as he learns about a boy who moved several times with mother and how each place he lived influenced his life. The Transformer symbolizes the themes of change and transformation that are prevalent throughout the book. Jin explains his background after the panel shows the family arriving at their new home.

Jin was born in Chinatown but moved to a suburb when he is nine. He was happy in Chinatown and fit in with easily with his peers. He went to the herbalist with his mother every week. One day, he tells the herbalist's wife that he wants to become a Transformer. She replies, "It's easy to become anything you wish … so long as you are willing to forfeit your soul." This statement is a warning that foreshadows future events.

After the move, Jin attends his new school, where there is only one other Asian student, Suzy Nakamura. He faces racial prejudice from his classmates, and his first friend, Peter, is really a bully who abuses Jin. When Jin is in fifth grade, Wei-Chen arrives from Taiwan. Jin initially dislikes

Wei-Chen because he is too Asian. Wei-Chen's English is broken, and he does not understand American culture. Jin refers to him as an F.O.B., which stands for *fresh off the boat*. Jin does not want to associate with someone who is a constant reminder of what makes him different from the other students. At first, Jin refuses to be friends with Wei-Chen. The boys soon bond, however, when Wei-Chen offers to let Jin see his robot that turns into a monkey. This scene is a reminder of Jin's love of Transformers and all that they represent. By the end of this section, Jin reveals that Wei-Chen is his best friend.

Danny and Chin-Kee

The next section of the book is called "Everyone Ruvs Chin-Kee." This is the only section of *American Born Chinese* with a title. It also has a laugh track and clapping at the bottom of different panels. There is no narrator; dialogue and pictures move the story forward. This comical farce is the story of Danny, a blonde, American teenager who is visited by his cousin Chin-Kee. Danny is studying with a girl he likes, Melanie, when his cousin arrives. She quickly leaves after Chin-Kee makes several insulting comments. Chin-Kee embodies every negative Chinese stereotype. Yang draws him differently from other Asian characters. His features are exaggerated and his clothing is nineteenth-century Chinese dress. He speaks with a severe accent and behaves inappropriately, embarrassing his cousin. On the surface, Chin-Kee is offensive, but Binbin Fu explains, in his review, that the character is an "effective way to dispel the century-old image of the 'Heathen Chinee.'"

Monkey King

Monkey King's second appearance shows how the rejection of the gods has affected him. Humiliated, he is determined to transform himself and the other monkeys. He begins by ordering all monkeys to wear shoes. The shoes make life more difficult for his subjects, who spend much of their time in trees. The Monkey King then locks himself away to study other Kung-Fu disciplines. He masters the four major disciplines of invulnerability and the four major disciplines of bodily form. Mastering these disciplines allows the Monkey King to change his size, clone himself, shape shift, and become invulnerable to injury and death. After attaining these powers, the Monkey King decides that he will no longer be a monkey and changes his name to the Great Sage, Equal of Heaven. He makes himself taller and appears more human.

When he returns to his subjects, the Monkey King learns that he has been sentenced to execution because of his attack in heaven. Monkey King goes to the Dragon King of the Eastern Sea, who is ordered to execute him. The Dragon King finds it impossible to execute the Monkey King because of his invulnerability. The Mon-key King takes on a larger form and attacks the Dragon King to convince him that he is no longer a monkey. In his defeat, the Dragon King gives the Monkey King a magic cudgel.

The Monkey King goes on to visit the sage Lao-Tzu, Yama of the Underworld, and the Jade Emperor of the Celestials. Each one laughs at the Monkey King, and each one is defeated by him. Afraid of the Monkey King's transformation, the deities and spirits beg the emissaries of Tze-Yo-Tzuh to ask him to save them from the Monkey King.

Tze-Yo-Tzuh, whose name means *He Who Is*, is a supreme being. He finds the Monkey King beating a human and asks why he is so angry. Tze-Yo-Tzuh reveals that he made the Monkey King, and he fully intended the monkey deity to be a monkey. He also explains that he is always with the Monkey King and knows everything he does. The Monkey King refuses to accept his own identity or Tze-Yo-Tzuh's. He tries to escape Tze-Yo-Tzuh and flies beyond the universe. There, he finds five gold pillars and marks one. He returns to tell Tze-Yo-Tzuh how he escaped his grasp, but Tze-Yo-Tzuh shows him a mark on his hand. The five gold pillars were Tze-Yo-Tzuh's fingers. Stubbornly determined to change his identity, the Monkey King attempts to fight Tze-Yo-Tzuh and is imprisoned under a pile of rocks for five hundred years. A seal on the rocks prevents the Monkey King from using Kung-Fu.

Jin

The next section of the novel returns to Jin's

story. Now in middle school, he develops a crush on his Caucasian classmate Amelia Harris. Jin confides his feelings to Wei-Chen, who laughs at him for falling in love so young. Jin reminds him that they are in America and that it is normal to date girls. Wei-Chen takes his advice and begins dating the other Asian American student, Suzy Nakamura. Jin finds it impossible to talk with the girl of his dreams and convinces himself that she likes another boy, Greg. Jin copies Greg's hairstyle to make himself more appealing. The curly hairstyle does not suit Jin just as the shoes do not suit the monkeys. As Jin and his friends handle typical teenage problems, they suffer racial slurs from other students.

Wei-Chen and Amelia take care of animals for science class, and they accidentally lock themselves in a supply closet one day. While they are alone together, Wei-Chen tells Amelia what a good friend Jin is to him. Amelia is impressed by Wei-Chen's story, and asks him if Jin likes her. When Jin lets them out of the closet, Wei-Chen tells him to ask Amelia out. Jin finally has the courage to make his feelings known, and Amelia agrees to go out with him.

Danny and Chin-Kee

The second installment of Danny and Chin-Kee takes place in Danny's high school. Again, Chin-Kee exhibits the worst Asian stereotypes. He obnoxiously answers all of the questions in class. He talks about eating cat. He quotes proverbs and talks about finding an American wife. He even plays a disgusting joke on Danny's friend Steve, explaining that he does it because he is Chinese. By the end of the day, the other students are mocking Chin-Kee and avoiding Danny. Danny confides in Steve that he is forced to change schools every year after Chin-Kee visits because, "by the time he leaves, no one thinks of me as Danny anymore. I'm Chin-Kee's cousin." Danny's anger is visible by the end of this section.

Monkey King

The story of the Monkey King continues after a five-hundred–year break. It begins with the history of Wong Lai-Tsao, who is one of the four monks to achieve legendary status. He is only impressive in one way: he spends every day feeding and helping the vagrants outside town. He does this faithfully even though the vagrants do not appreciate him. One day, a vagrant asks Wong Lai-Tsao why he helps them. The monk replies that Tze-Yo-Tzuh loves him and he must share that love. The vagrants transform into the emissaries of Tze-Yo-Tzuh after Wong-Lai-Tsao answers. The emissaries tell Wong Lai-Tsao that Tze-Yo-Tzuh wishes him to travel to the West with three gifts. If he accepts the mission, he will be in danger from demons who believe eating a monk will make them immortal. He will also have three disciples, and one of his disciples will be the Monkey King.

The monk accepts the mission and travels to

find the Monkey King under the mountain of rock. Wong Lai-Tsao tells the Monkey King that Tze-Yo-Tzuh wants him to be his disciple, and he must free himself from the rock. The Monkey King still refuses to be a monkey, insisting that he is the Great Sage, Equal of Heaven. He reminds Wong Lai-Tsao that he cannot free himself because Tze-Yo-Tzuh placed a seal on the rock preventing the Monkey King from using Kung-Fu. Wong Lai-Tsao explains that if he releases his Kung-Fu and takes his true form, the Monkey King will be small enough to free himself.

The panels show demons following the monk. The Monkey King refuses to return to his true form, and he tells Wong Lai-Tsao that he will watch the demons eat him. As the demons attack, the monk tells the Monkey King that this is his last chance for freedom. At the final moment, the Monkey King takes his true form and escapes. He saves Wong Lai-Tsao from the demons using Kung-Fu. He accepts his role as the monk's disciple and agrees to help him on the journey to the West. Wong Lai-Tsao makes one final demand of the Monkey King. He must give up his shoes before starting the mission. The Monkey King leaves his shoes behind and begins his journey to the West. By leaving his shoes, he is fully relinquishing his identity as the Great Sage, Equal of Heaven.

Jin

Jin is excited about his date with Amelia, but

he has a problem. He is not allowed to date because his parents want him to focus on his schoolwork. Jin plans to tell his mother that he is studying at Wei-Chen's house and convinces Wei-Chen to lie if his mother calls looking for him. Wei-Chen is not comfortable with lying and only agrees out of his loyalty to Jin. Readers later learn that lying goes against his oath to Tze-Yo-Tzuh.

On his date with Amelia, Jin recalls dating instructions from his older cousin, Charlie. He takes Amelia to the movies on his bike and is sweating when they arrive. His parents do not buy deodorant, and he remembers his cousin's advice to use restroom soap under his arms when out with a girl. Jin follows this advice, but is horrified when he realizes that he left soap bubbles on Amelia's shoulder after putting his arm around her. As they leave the movie, Greg is watching them in the picture.

The next day, Jin is worried that Amelia did not enjoy their date. Wei-Chen attempts to help Jin by asking Amelia if she had a good time. She does not mention noticing the soap bubbles, and she tells Wei-Chen that she had fun. Jin is happy and dreams about his future with Amelia until Greg talks to him. Greg asks Jin not to go out with Amelia again because "she has to start paying attention to who she hangs out with." Flustered by the request, Jin reluctantly agrees, but he fantasizes about telling Greg no and hitting him. When he does run into Greg and Amelia, he does not say anything.

Angry and humiliated, Jin finds Suzy crying

alone on the street. She tells him about being ignored by an old friend at a party and a boy, Timmy, calling her a racial slur. She admits that she feels like a foreigner all the time. Jin kisses Suzy when she is vulnerable. She becomes angry and hits him before running away.

Jin has an ice pack on his face when Wei-Chen comes over. He asks Jin why he would betray him and kiss his girlfriend. Wei-Chen tells Jin that they are brothers because they are alike, but this reminds Jin of what makes him different. Jin lashes out at Wei-Chen instead of the people who discriminated against him. He calls Wei-Chen a F.O.B. and tells him that he is not good enough for Suzy. Wei-Chen punches Jin before leaving.

That night, Jin dreams of the herbalist's wife. She asks him what he would like to become, and he transforms into Danny. Jin wakes up to see Danny's face in the mirror. Jin is happy, but the figure of the herbalist's wife indicates that the transformation has cost Jin his soul.

Danny and Chin-Kee

Danny finds Chin-Kee dancing and singing on a table in the library, in the final installment of their story. Some students comment that he is spitting and that they need to be tested for the SARS virus. Danny drags his cousin out of the library and tells him to go back to China. Chin-Kee refuses, and Danny begins to hit him. Chin-Kee warns Danny to stop, but Danny refuses. The boys fight, and Chin-

Kee beats up Danny, telling him that he will stay in America forever. Danny then hits Chin-Kee so hard that his head falls off, revealing the Monkey King.

The Monkey King tells Danny that they should both take their true forms, and Danny turns back into Jin. The Monkey King reveals that Wei-Chen was really his son sent by Tze-Yo-Tzuh as an emissary. Wei-Chen initially valued his friendship with Jin, but later decided that humans are "petty, soulless creatures." This comment reminds readers that Jin had to lose his soul to transform into Danny. After Jin's betrayal, Wei-Chen chooses to spend his time on earth living for pleasure.

Jin believes that the Monkey King used Chin-Kee to punish him for Wei-Chen's disobedience, but the Monkey King explains that he was only acting as Jin's conscience. He wants Jin to accept himself for who he is. Jin retains his true form after encountering the Monkey King. By seeing himself clearly, Jin regains his soul and begins an internal transformation. The Monkey King leaves Jin, and a card for a bakery falls into Jin's hand. Jin returns home and tells his mother and father that Chin-Kee is gone. Each parent has assumed that Chin-Kee was the other's nephew.

Jin goes to the bakery on the card every day for a month. Finally, a transformed Wei-Chen drives up to the bakery. He looks more Americanized. He is smoking and no longer speaks broken English, but his language is coarse. Initially, he is rude and angry with Jin. Jin, however, tells Wei-Chen that he saw his father and wants to talk to him. They order pearl milk tea, and Jin apologizes to Wei-Chen. Wei-Chen does not immediately accept his apology, but he offers to take Jin to a place that serves better pearl milk tea.

The final picture in the book appears after the end of the story. It is one of Jin and Wei-Chen as the Back Dorm Boys, according to Yang's interview with Sunny Woan. This is a pop-culture reference to the popular online video. The Back Dorm Boys are two Chinese students in a dorm who lip-synch American pop songs.

Characters

Charlie

Jin's older cousin, Charlie, is a minor character. He only appears in Jin's memory. Jin remembers all of Charlie's advice about dating. Charlie is the one who tells Jin about using the soap in public restrooms as deodorant.

Chin-Kee

Chin-Kee is introduced to readers as Danny's cousin from China. He is a negative Chinese stereotype whose offensive behavior humiliates Danny and alienates him from his friends. At the climax, Chin-Kee is revealed as the Monkey King in disguise. He masquerades as Chin-Kee to be Danny's, or Jin's, conscience.

Danny

Danny is a blond, all-American high school student who is embarrassed each year when his cousin Chin-Kee comes to visit. Every year Danny changes schools because of his cousin. At the climax of the story, the readers learns that Danny is really Jin transformed.

Demons

Wong Lai-Tsao is attacked by nameless demons when he first meets the Monkey King. The demons believe that eating a monk will make them live forever. The Monkey King escapes from the mountain of rocks and uses his Kung-Fu skills to save Wong Lai-Tsao from the demons.

Dragon King of the Eastern Sea

The Dragon King of the Eastern Sea is a Chinese deity. He is instructed to execute the Monkey King for his assault on heaven. The Dragon King of the Eastern Sea, however, cannot kill the Monkey King because of his invulnerability. After being defeated by the Monkey King, the Dragon King of the Eastern Sea gives him a magic cudgel.

Emissaries of Tze-Yo-Tzuh

The original servants of Tze-Yo-Tzuh are the ox, the eagle, the lion, and the human. They communicate messages to and from Tze-Yo-Tzuh. They give Tze-Yo-Tzuh the message from the gods and tell Wong Lai-Tsao about his mission to the West. The Monkey King later calls himself an emissary of Tze-Yo-Tzuh. Wei-Chen briefly serves as an emissary of Tze-Yo-Tzuh, but he abandons his mission.

Greg

Greg is a blond student with curly hair in the

same class as Jin and Wei-Chen Sun. He is a friend of Timmy's, but he does not call Jin and his friends racial slurs. He will not, however, do anything to stop Timmy and another boy from insulting Jin, Suzy, and Wei-Chen Sun. Jin is jealous of Greg's friendship with Amelia and copies Greg's hairstyle to impress her. Greg asks Jin to stay away from Amelia because being seen out with Jin is not good for her reputation.

Amelia Harris

Amelia is a pretty, blonde classmate of Jin's and his eighth grade crush. She does not share the prejudices of some of the other students and even goes on a date with Jin. She likes Jin, but Jin allows her friend, Greg, to come between them.

Herbalist's Wife

A name is never given for the herbalist's wife in Chinatown, but she is important to the story. She tells Jin that he can become anything if he will sacrifice his soul. She appears in Jin's dream before he transforms into Danny.

Jade Emperor

The Jade Emperor of the Celestials does not believe that the Monkey King is a threat until he faces the Monkey King's magic cudgel. After being defeated by the Monkey King, the Jade Emperor and other deities complain to the emissaries of Tze-

Yo-Tzuh and ask for help.

Wong Lai-Tsao

As one of the four legendary monks, Wong Lai-Tsao has only one attribute that makes him legendary: he can share the love of his creator. Wong Lai-Tsao consistently loves and cares for vagrants who are not kind to him. The vagrants transform into the emissaries of Tze-Yo-Tzuh after testing him. They inform him that Tze-Yo-Tzuh has a mission for him to travel West with three disciples. The first disciple Wong Lai-Tsao finds is the Monkey King trapped under the rock mountain. Wong Lai-Tsao teaches the Monkey King how to accept his true identity and free himself from the mountain of rocks.

Lao-Tzu

Lao-Tzu is a sage and patron of immortality. He laughs at the Monkey King for saying that he is no longer a monkey. Lao-Tzu grows afraid of the Monkey King after he uses his shape-shifting ability.

Melanie

Melanie is a girl Danny likes. He is studying with her when Chin-Kee arrives. After meeting Chin-Kee, she tells Danny that she only wants to be friends and says that he has buck teeth.

Monkey King

The Monkey King is a popular character from Chinese folktales. The story of the Monkey King has been in print since the sixteenth-century book *Journey to the West*. Yang borrows elements from the traditional story for his graphic novel but alters a few details. In this story, the Monkey King is born from a rock and becomes the ruler and deity of the monkeys on Flower-Fruit Mountain. He masters Kung-Fu disciplines, including the four heavenly disciplines that make him immortal. The Monkey King is happy until he attempts to enter a banquet of the gods. He is not allowed inside because he is a monkey and because he has no shoes. He grows ashamed of being a monkey.

The Monkey King transforms himself by mastering the major disciplines of invulnerability and the four major disciplines of bodily form. The disciplines of invulnerability make him impervious to harm, and the disciplines of bodily form allow him to change his shape and size and clone himself. Having mastered all of the Kung-Fu disciplines, the Monkey King calls himself the Great Sage, Equal of Heaven and makes himself physically larger and more intimidating. He is sentenced to death for attacking the other gods, but he cannot be killed. The Monkey King attacks the deities who laughed at him to prove that he is no longer a monkey.

The Monkey King refuses to listen to Tze-Yo-Tzuh, his creator, and insists that he is the Great Sage, Equal of Heaven. He is trapped under a mountain of rocks for five hundred years after trying to fight Tze-Yo-Tzuh, who places a seal on the rocks to prevent the Monkey King from practicing Kung-Fu. The Monkey King becomes the disciple of the monk Wong Lai-Tsao and escapes the mountain when he learns to accept himself as a monkey. The Monkey King later becomes the emissary of Tze-Yo-Tzuh and the father of Wei-Chen Sun. He also masquerades as Danny's cousin, Chin-Kee.

Suzy Nakamura

Suzy is a Japanese American student in the same class as Jin and Wei-Chen. She dates Wei-Chen Sun, and she punches Jin after he kisses her.

Peter

Peter is Jin's first friend at school. Peter is a bully who demands that Jin be his friend. He is abusive and plays cruel games with Jin. He leaves one summer and does not return.

Steve

Steve is Danny's friend. They are on the basketball team together. Chin-Kee plays a joke on Steve that eventually drives them apart.

Wei-Chen Sun

Wei-Chen Sun emigrates from Taiwan and

joins Jin's class in the fifth grade. Jin initially rejects Wei-Chen's friendship. Wei-Chen speaks broken English at first. He has a robot that transforms into a monkey, and Jin bonds with Wei-Chen Sun over the robot. Wei-Chen soon becomes Jin's most loyal friend. He dates Suzy Nakamura and ends his friendship with Jin after Jin kisses her.

At the end of the story, he is revealed to be the son of the Monkey King sent as an ambassador by Tze-Yo-Tzuh. He refuses to follow his mission after Jin betrays him, and he seeks to please only himself. His appearance and manner of speaking change to illustrate how his anger and selfish behavior have negatively affected him. Jin eventually finds Wei-Chen Sun and apologizes to him at the end of the story.

Timmy

Timmy is a boy whom Jin encounters on his first day at his new school. He is quick to make racist comments about Jin. He continues his abuse over the years. In middle school, he calls Suzy a racial slur that makes her cry.

Tze-Yo-Tzuh

Tze-Yo-Tzuh is a supreme being and creator of all things, including the gods. When the Monkey King becomes too powerful, the gods turn to Tze-Yo-Tzuh's emissaries and ask for his help. Tze-Yo-Tzuh tries to reason with the Monkey King but has to trap him under a mountain of rocks when the Monkey King attacks him. He later sends Wei-Chen as an emissary to humanity.

Jin Wang

Jin is a young Chinese American boy who moves from San Francisco's Chinatown to the suburbs. He plays with Transformers as a young child in Chinatown, and he wishes to become one. As one of only three Asian American students in a suburban school, he faces racial prejudice and stereotyping. He tries to fit in with his Caucasian peers, but he is not fully accepted by most of them.

Jin initially dislikes Wei-Chen Sun because he is new to America, but they soon bond over transforming robots and become best friends. In the eighth grade, Jin develops a crush on Amelia Harris and changes his hair to look more American. He goes on one date with Amelia thanks to the help of Wei-Chen. The date goes well, but another student, Greg, asks Jin to stay away from Amelia for the sake of her reputation.

Jin is frustrated by the prejudice he faces and kisses Suzy, Wei-Chen Sun's girlfriend, in an emotional moment. He lashes out at Wei-Chen when confronted and ends their friendship. Jin eventually transforms into Danny, who is tormented by his Chinese cousin Chin-Kee. Jin returns to his true form after encountering the Monkey King.

Mrs. Wang

Jin's mother tells him stories of the Monkey King.

Yama

As the caretaker of the underworld, Yama is an important deity. Monkey King uses his ability to turn his hair into clones to convince Yama that he is no longer a monkey but the Great Sage Equal of Heaven.

Themes

Self Identity

The two main characters in *American Born Chinese* have trouble accepting their personal identities. In a sense, the characters feel trapped between two worlds. Both Jin and the Monkey King suffer rejection because they are different. In an attempt to conform and be accepted, each one rejects a part of himself. The Monkey King is both a monkey and a deity, but he refuses to be identified as a monkey. He wishes to be only the Great Sage, Equal of Heaven. He changes his form and wears shoes to become someone else. Jin is a Chinese American who rejects his Chinese heritage to transform into the Caucasian American, Danny.

Both Jin and the Monkey King face their greatest struggles by rejecting their personal identities. They only find peace by accepting who and what they truly are. The Monkey King is released from his prison of rock by reverting into his true form as a monkey. Danny ends his humiliation at the hands of Chin-Kee when he confronts his fear of being stereotyped as Asian and again becomes Jin.

Stereotypes

Stereotypes are commonly used in comics and

graphic novels because "everything in comic books, including character, is reduced to two-dimensional images," as Randy Duncan and Matthew J. Smith point out in *The Power of Comics: History, Form, and Culture*. Early comics often featured unflattering stereotypes of minority characters. The character Chin-Kee is an extreme stereotype who reflects the early Western caricatures of Chinese people. His name is also a play on a negative term for Chinese individuals. At first glance, Chin-Kee is offensive, but Yang uses the character to turn the stereotype on its head.

Topics for Further Study

- Read *The Absolutely True Diary of a Part-Time Indian*, Sherman Alexie's young-adult novel about a Native American teenager, Arnold Spirit, who faces the challenges of being Native American, poor, and mentally challenged. This 2007 National Book Award winner is a narrative mixed with cartoons that the main character draws to explore his feelings. Compare and contrast this book with *American Born Chinese* in an essay. How are the themes, characters, and use of graphics similar? How are they different?

- Research the history of comics and graphic novels from the 1960s to the present. Create a video or multimedia presentation that shows the changes in form, subject matter, and critical reception. Include Yang's work in this presentation, and point out the specific techniques used in *American Born Chinese* and his other comic art. Complete your presentation by speculating on the future of the medium.

- In "Origins of American Born Chinese—part 1" (available at http://firstsecondbooks.typepad.com/mai Yang wrote, "The Monkey King is universal." Read the book *Monkey: A Folk Novel of China*, and study the different representations of the Monkey King over the centuries. Create an original story involving the Monkey King and include illustrations. You may write a narrative, draw a comic, or create a Web comic.

- Explore the history of Asian American art. Create a Web page providing an overview of Asian American art and artists that includes different genres. Provide a brief biography for each artist and incorporate links to examples of his or her art. Be sure to include Yang in your Web page.

Chin-Kee's extreme behavior is so stereotypical that he becomes unbelievable. He represents Danny's, or Jin's, greatest fears about being Chinese in America. The author explains the purpose of Chin-Kee in the "Origins of ABC—part 3" when he notes that "in order for us to defeat our enemy, he must first be made visible." By exposing the stereotype as ludicrous, Yang reveals it for the farce that it is and removes its power.

Transformation

Transformation is an underlying theme throughout *American Born Chinese*, as Fu and other critics point out. In this story, transformation is not always positive. The different characters learn how to transform themselves both inside and out. Physical transformation, however, does not lead to maturity, enlightenment, or peace. The Monkey King masters the disciplines of bodily form as part of an effort to change himself from the Monkey King to the Great Sage, Equal of Heaven. He is able to change physically but inside he remains the same. The true transformation of the Monkey King occurs when he learns to accept himself and return to his true physical form.

Transformation is a concept essentially linked to Jin's character. As a child, Jin's favorite toy is a Transformer, and he bonds with Wei-Chen over a transforming robot. These toys are images of his desire to change. Jin loves Transformers so much that he wants to be one when he grows up. The herbalist's wife gives Jin the secret of becoming a transformer before he moves to the suburbs: "It's easy to become anything you wish … so long as you are willing to forfeit your soul." After betraying Wei-Chen, Jin physically transforms into Danny. Danny, however, has the same anger and fear that Jin had before the transformation. Danny confronts his feelings of fear and anger at the climax of the story, and the Monkey King returns Jin to his true physical form. Jin begins a journey toward self-acceptance, which leads to an internal transformation.

Wei Chen's transformation is more complex than the transformations of the other characters. He is physically transformed by Tze-Yo-Tzuh to serve as an emissary on earth. This transformation from a monkey to a human does not negatively affect Wei-Chen. He is a positive character until Jin betrays their friendship. Wei-Chen remains human after the betrayal, but he takes on a negative transformation after ending his friendship with Jin. He abandons his mission, speaks coarsely, dresses differently, and smokes.

Graphic Novel

American Born Chinese is considered a graphic novel. Graphic novel is a term used to describe literary works drawn in the same style as comic books. The main difference between comic books and graphic novels is their length. Both comic books and graphic novels employ sequential art. In sequential art, pictures of specific moments are called panels, as Duncan and Smith explain. The panels are placed in a specific order to illustrate a sequence of events. Most comics add text in the form of narration or dialogue to the assist with the plot.

Comic books are usually serialized, meaning that each comic book tells a portion of the story. Terms for longer or complete comic stories were discussed as early as the 1960s; however, Will Eisner made the term graphic novel popular with his 1978 book *Contract with God and other Tenement Stories*, according to Stephen Weiner in "Pioneer and Storyteller: The Graphic Novels of Will Eisner." Eisner is considered by experts such as Weiner to be the father of the graphic novel.

Yang's *American Born Chinese* has all of the attributes of a graphic novel. It uses the style of a comic book to complete this multi-narrative story. The book was originally serialized online at *Modern*

Tales.com, but it is now published in the graphic-novel format.

Multi-narrative

American Born Chinese is a complex, multi-narrative text that explores different stories as well as different points of view within each narrative. Each story is unique. Jin's story is told in the first person, while the Monkey King has an omniscient narrator. Danny and Chin-Kee are not narrated. Their story relies on dialogue and resembles a sitcom script with laughing and clapping at the bottom of some panels. The separate stories effectively come together at the climax of the book to give the readers a clear understanding of all the events.

Intertextuality

A Handbook to Literature notes that Julia Kristeva (an influential modern-day French literary critic and philosopher) coined the term intertextuality. The term applies when one text echoes another in any way. This can occur when someone borrows a story, quotes a line, creates a parody, or alludes to another text. For example, poets sometimes quote other authors or allude to classical stories in their work. Intertextuality appears on different scales. They can be a few words or permeate the entire narrative. *American Born Chinese* applies intertextuality on a large scale by adopting the traditional tale of the Monkey King.

Yang, however, alters the details and focus of the character from the *Journey to the West* to fit his narrative and worldview. For example, he removes the elements of political satire found in the novel.

Asian American History

Asian Americans are Americans of Asian descent. The term technically applies to families from all parts of Asia. Most Americans, however, associate the term with people whose ancestors are from East Asia, such as China and Japan, because Yuji Ichioka developed the term in the 1960s as an alternative to the word Oriental, according to K. Connie Kang's obituary for Ichioka in the *Los Angeles Times*.

Asian Americans are an integral part of American culture. According to the "Timeline of Asian American History" on the *Digital History* Web site, there was a Filipino settlement in Louisiana before the American Revolution, and Chinese and Japanese sailors landed in Hawaii in the early nineteenth century. Unfortunately, the rights of Asians have been limited in American history. For example, the Naturalization Act of 1790 restricted citizenship to Caucasian Americans.

A significant number of Chinese and Japanese immigrants began arriving in the United States in the 1840s in response to the Gold Rush. Hikozo Hamada was the first Japanese man to be naturalized as an American citizen in 1850, but many Americans feared granting citizenship to Asians. Citizenship and rights for Asians were limited even after the Fourteenth Amendment granted citizenship to former slaves. The Naturalization Act of 1870, for example, denied citizenship to Chinese laborers and did not allow their wives to join them. The Chinese Exclusion Act of 1882 essentially prevented the entry of new Chinese laborers and repealed any state laws that would naturalize individuals from China.

Fear of an unknown culture created stereotypes of Chinese Americans in the nineteenth century that Fu, in a MELUS article, calls the *Heathen Chinee*. Different states within the United States created anti-miscegenation laws, which prohibited marriage between Chinese and other Asians with Americans. Deenesh Sohoni points out in *Law & Society Review* that these laws persisted into the early twentieth century.

To counter the fear of Asians in America, social scientists between 1910 and 1960 focused on the assimilation of Asians into Western society, as Sucheng Chan explains in "The Writing of Asian American History." Despite these efforts, many Americans considered all Asians to be foreigners. World War II saw the relocation of Japanese Americans to internment camps. Despite this discrimination, the Japanese 442nd Regimental Combat Team was the most decorated American unit during the war.

The 1960s saw the rise of civil rights support. The civil rights movement affected different minorities in America and signaled a turning point for Asian American rights. The term Asian

American, as we know it, was coined, and colleges began including ethnic studies programs. Asian Americans were elected to office and served as judges, and laws protecting the rights of immigrants were created.

Chan considers the 1980s to be the decade when "Asian American historiography is finally coming of age." The Civil Liberties Act of 1988 made reparations for Japanese Americans interred during World War II. The rights of Asian American are now guaranteed. Centuries of stereotyping Asian cultures, however, have left an impression on American perception. In his graphic novel, Yang addresses these stereotypes and the challenges Asian Americans still face.

Comics and Graphic Novel History

Sequential art, or a series of pictures that tell a story, has been used for centuries. Experts such as Duncan and Smith, however, consider Rodolphe Tölpffer to be the father of the comic book because of the picture stories he created between 1827 and 1844. Soon after, popular comic strips mirroring Tölpffer's technique began to appear in the newspapers. The *Yellow Kid*, for example, was released in 1863, and the comics were later reprinted into books.

The modern form of the comic book was seen in 1929 with *The Funnies*. Comic books became a popular form of entertainment in the United States in the 1930s and 1940s. Comic books developed into different genres beyond humor to include adventure, detective fiction, and superhero fiction. The 1950s saw a decline in the demand for comic books. As American households acquired televisions, fewer comic books were sold. There was also a backlash against comic books with explicit subject matter after *The Seduction of the Innocent: The Influence of Comic Books on Today's Youth* was released in 1954. A Senate subcommittee investigated the effect of comics on delinquent behavior the same year. In response to public concern, the Code of the Comics Magazine Association was created. The Association's seal indicated that comic books were suitable for children.

The 1960s and 1970s saw a move away from commercialism in the comic book industry. Comics developed as an art form that focused on literary themes. The appeal of underground and independent publishers grew during this time. The term *graphic novel* was created to describe book-length comics and was applied to Eisner's 1978 text, *Contract with God and other Tenement Stories.*

Graphic novels and comics became appreciated as literature in the 1980s and 1990s. *Maus, The Watchmen*, and *The Dark Knight Returns* were published in 1986 and "won attention in the popular press," as Duncan and Smith point out. Critical appreciation for graphic novels developed in the 1990s, and *Maus II* won a special Pulitzer Prize in 1992. Respect for graphic novels and comics continues to grow in the twenty-first century. They are embraced in classrooms and still draw critical acclaim; *American Born Chinese*, for example, is the first graphic novel to be nominated for the National Book Award.

Critical Overview

American Born Chinese was physically published in 2006 and became Yang's first profitable work as a comic writer and artist. The reviews have been overwhelmingly positive. Most critics quickly noticed the importance of the book's subject matter in modern American society. Jesse Karp, in *Booklist*, notes that "the stories have a simple, engaging sweep to them, but their weighty subjects—shame, racism, and friendship—receive thoughtful, powerful examination." In the *Journal of Adolescent & Adult Literacy*, Michael D. Boatright praises the relevance of *American Born Chinese* and how it relates to "immigrant identity issues."

Some critics immediately applauded Yang's strong narrative ability, while others found the multi-narrative approach unappealing. In his review of *American Born Chinese* for MELUS, Fu opines that "what makes it especially appealing to both young and mature readers is its narrative depth." He calls the climax "cleverly woven together." Ned Vizzini, in the *New York Times*, however, argues that the book is "hampered by a confusing ending that stretches to resolve the three tales."

In a graphic novel, the quality of the drawing and color choices is important. Critics have predominantly united over the visual appeal of *American Born Chinese*, praising its simplicity and use of color. A contributor to the *Bulletin of the Center for Children's Books* comments that "the palette is softly muted, so that even the strongest colors in the action scenes never reach the intensity of a visual assault." Fu also calls it "mature in artistic design and visually engaging."

What Do I Read Next?

- Tanuja Desai Hidier's work of young-adult fiction, *Born Confused*, was published in 2002. This is the story of Dimple Lala, an American teenager who, like Yang's characters, struggles between two worlds. Dimple is an Indian American who attempts to fit in with both her family and American peers as she discovers who she is.

- *The Chinese in America: A Narrative History* (2006) by Iris

Chang is a historical account of Chinese immigration to America in the nineteenth and twentieth centuries, as well as the resistance immigrants faced. By employing a narrative style, Chang makes it easier for the readers to understand the historical events that led to the cultural setting of *American Born Chinese*.

- Yang followed *American Born Chinese* by collaborating with Derek Kirk Kim in the 2009 young-adult graphic novel *The Eternal Smile: Three Stories*. The stories in this book differ from Yang's previous work by exploring the connection between fantasy and reality.

- Stephen Weiner's *Faster Than a Speeding Bullet: The Rise of the Graphic Novel* (2003) provides a historic look at the rise of popular comics and graphic novels. The nonfiction account looks at graphic novels as part of the general publishing industry.

- Art Spiegelman first published *Maus I: A Survivor's Tale: My Father Bleeds History* in 1986. This novel-length work of sequential art, based on the events of the Holocaust, was one of the first graphic novels accepted as mainstream literature. The second installment, *Maus II: A Survivor's Tale: And Here My Troubles Began*, won a special Pulitzer Prize in 1992 and helped pave the way for other comic artists and writers to be taken seriously. This dark story contrasts with *American Born Chinese* and shows the versatility of the comic medium.

- Edited by Keith Lawrence and Floyd Cheung, *Recovered Legacies: Authority and Identity in Early Asian American Literature* (2005) is a collection of essays that examine early Asian American literature and its influence on culture and identity. The essays address little-known Asian American stories that, like *American Born Chinese*, reflect the experiences of Asian Americans throughout history.

Sources

American Born Chinese Reviews, in *First Second Books.com*, http://www.firstsecondbooks.com/reviews/reviewsA (accessed July 15, 2011); originally published in *Bulletin of the Center for Children's Books*, November 2006.

"American Born Chinese—Reviews, in *First Second Books.com*, http://www.firstsecondbooks.com/reviews/reviewsA (accessed July 15, 2011); originally published in *School Library Journal*, September 2006.

Boatright, Michael D., "Graphic Journeys: Graphic Novels' Representations of Immigrant Experiences," in *Journal of Adolescent & Adult Literacy*, Vol. 53, No. 6, March 2010, pp. 468–76.

Chan, Sucheng, "The Writing of Asian American History," in *OAH Magazine of History*, Vol. 10, No. 4, Summer 1996, pp. 8–17.

Duncan, Randy, and Matthew J. Smith, *The Power of Comics: History Form and Culture*, Continuum International Publishing, 2009, pp. 25–26, 71, 135.

Fu, Binbin, Review of *American Born Chinese*, in *MELUS*, Vol. 32, No. 3, Fall 2007, pp. 274–76.

Garrity, Shaenon, "The History of Webcomics," in *Comics Journal*, http://www.tcj.com/the-history-of-webcomics/ (accessed July 15, 2011).

"Gene Yang Biography," in *Gene Yang Home Page*, http://wn.com/Gene_Yang (accessed on July 15, 2011).

"Intertextuality," in *A Handbook to Literature*, 9th ed., edited by William Harmon and Hugh Holman, Prentice Hall, 2003, p. 268.

Kang, K., Connie, "Yuji Ichioka, 66; Led Way in Studying Lives of Asian Americans," in *UCLA Asian American Studies Center*, http://www.aasc.ucla.edu/archives/yuji66latimes.asp (accessed July 20, 2011); originally published in *Los Angeles Times*, September 7, 2002.

Karp, Jesse, Review of *American Born Chinese*, in *Booklist Online*, http://www.booklistonline.com/American-Born-Chinese-Gene-Luen-Yang/pid=1735514 (accessed July 14, 2011).

Review of *American Born Chinese*, in *First Second Books.com*, http://www.firstsecondbooks.com/reviews/reviewsA (accessed July 15, 2011); originally published in *Bulletin of the Center for Children's Books*, November 2006.

Sohoni, Deenesh, "Unsuitable Suitors: Anti-Miscegenation Laws, Naturalization Laws, and the Construction of Asian Identities," in *Law and Society Review*, Vol. 41, No. 3, September 2007, pp. 587–618.

"Timeline of Asian American History," in *Digital History*,

http://www.digitalhistory.uh.edu/asian_voices/asian_ (accessed July 25, 2011).

Vizzini, Ned, "High Anxiety," in *New York Times Sunday Book Review*, May 13, 2007, http://www.nytimes.com/2007/05/13/books/review/\ t.html? sq=Gene%20Yang%20and%20American%20Born% 5lmbfCp9/IlsX3/x8f2ODg (accessed July 13, 2011).

Weiner, Stephen, "Pioneer and Storyteller: The Graphic Novels of Will Eisner," in *The Will Eisner Companion: The Pioneering Spirit of the Father of the Graphic Novel*, D. C. Comics, 2004, pp. 107–110.

Woan, Sunny, "Interview with Gene Yang: Author of American Born Chinese," in *Kartika Review*, http://www.kartikareview.com/issue1/1gene.html (accessed July 12, 2011).

Yang, Gene, "About Gene Yang," in *Humble Comics.com*, http://geneyang.com/about (accessed on July 12, 2011).

———, *American Born Chinese*, colored by Lark Pien, First Second, 2006.

———, "Origins of American Born Chinese—part 1," in *First Second Weblog*, http://firstsecondbooks.typepad.com/mainblog/2006/ (accessed July 15, 2011).

———, "Origins of American Born Chinese—part 3," in *First Second Weblog*, http://firstsecondbooks.typepad.com/mainblog/2006/ (accessed July 15, 2011).

Further Reading

Lee, Jennifer, and Min Zhou, eds., *Asian American Youth: Culture, Identity and Ethnicity*, Routledge Press, 2004.

> This book is a collection of essays that study the effects of immigration and assimilation on young people from Asia in America. The concepts of ethnicity, multiculturalism, and personal identity reflect Yang's themes.

McCloud, Scott, *Making Comics: Storytelling Secrets of Comics, Manga and Graphic Novels*, Harper Paperbacks, 2006.

> McCloud uses the comic book format to describe how comics are made. This book is useful for anyone who wants a better understanding of the comic genre or who is interested in attempting sequential art.

Okihiro, Gary, *The Columbia Guide to Asian American History*, Columbia University Press, 2001.

> Professor Okihiro examines more than two hundred years of Asian American history and culture. A useful introduction to Asian American studies, this book includes

narratives that explore the Asian American experience.

Wright, Bradford W., *Comic Book Nation: The Transformation of Youth Culture in America*, Johns Hopkins University Press, 2001.

This nonfiction book explores how the comic genre reflects American history and society. Wright also touches on the influence comic books have on American culture.

Yang, Gene and Thiem Pham, *Level Up*, First Second, 2011.

Yang's young-adult graphic novel collaboration with Pham examines the idea of national identity, personal identity, and rebellion. While this book shares the theme of personal identity with *American Born Chinese*, it expands on the conflict between parental expectations and personal choice.

Suggested Search Terms

Gene Yang

American Born Chinese

Asian American history

Gene Yang AND American Born Chinese

graphic novel AND history

comics AND graphic novels

The Monkey King

Asian American culture

American Born Chinese AND criticism

Gene Yang AND criticism

Gene Yang AND graphic novel

CPSIA information can be obtained
at www.ICGtesting.com
Printed in the USA
BVHW08s0721100918
526997BV00018B/224/P

9 781375 375900